Hasta Mañana
A SPANISH MEMOIR

Nan Twynham

Published 2013 by arima publishing
www.arimapublishing.com

ISBN 978 1 84549 596 1
© Nan Twynham 2013

All rights reserved

This book is copyright. Subject to statutory exception and to provisions of relevant collective licensing agreements, no part of this publication may be reproduced, stored in a retrieval system, or transmitted in any form or by any means, without the prior written permission of the author.

Printed and bound in the United Kingdom
Typeset in Garamond

This book is sold subject to the conditions that it shall not, by way of trade or otherwise, be lent, re-sold, hired out, or otherwise circulated without the publisher's prior consent in any form of binding or cover other than that which it is published and without a similar condition including this condition being imposed on the subsequent purchaser.

Swirl is an imprint of arima publishing.

arima publishing
ASK House, Northgate Avenue
Bury St Edmunds, Suffolk IP32 6BB
t: (+44) 01284 700321
www.arimapublishing.com

Last Word First

How can a country that produced such sublime architecture as the enchanting Alhambra in Granada, Seville's splendid cathedral and soaring Giralda clock tower-and in the 20th century the idiosyncratic and wonderful La Pedrera and Casa Batllo in Barcelona, creations from the genius of Antoni Gaudi, also be responsible for the ruination of so many traditional inland villages as well as the despoliation of a large part of the coastline?

Benivergel in the Marina Alta region is a prime example. In the year 2000 it was a village of some 1,600 souls, with two butchers, two bakers, two hairdressers, a general store, a tobacconist, a garage and no less than seven bars.

Oh, and a post office – open mornings only – plus a small police station (*Guardia Civil*).

That was then, when we bought our little house on the edge of the village. I suppose with hindsight – always a wonderful thing – we should have seen the writing on the wall when a splendid town hall was erected the following year, the plaza in front renovated and plans put in place for a library and meeting hall/community centre. What was going on?

Very soon, within the next two years, developers began their encroachment – old properties were demolished and in their place on almost every corner of each street, a phoenix rose, in the shape of a block of flats. The mayor had a vision of the future and this vision was becoming a nightmare! Upheaval and noise reigned, so much so that by autumn 2005 the village was unrecognisable. We decided to sell up and put the house on the market with the agents from whom we had bought it. However, no buyer appeared by Christmas and we had second thoughts – maybe we did not want to leave our sunny spot, so took it off.

But, by spring 2007 we were looking at seven cranes from our first floor terrace and listening to a cacophony of builders' noise from dawn to dusk. Two blocks were going up opposite our four houses, dwarfing them and cutting out light and sun. We could only imagine the quality of life when the 40-plus apartments were occupied, with the addition of cars, vans and motorcycles. So, up for sale went the house and this time a Spanish couple wanting to return to their roots – they were from the village – came up with an offer in July and by September we were able to organise our removal. We gave power of attorney to estate agent Alex who had sold us the place originally and left him in charge of Operation Exodus.

So, what next? For husband, France beckoned – a few miles across the Channel, hence more accessible by sea and air (all those regional airports!), with usually better weather than ours and more sunshine. We did not let the grass grow – by early September we had received the payment for the Spanish house and we could begin hunting for a replacement in France. The furniture had to go somewhere! After exhaustive trawling of websites and agents' adverts in magazines, we were ready to 'go for it'. The chosen area was the Poitou-Charentes department. And that is another story!

Escape To The Sun

A song lyric from yesteryear: "This nearly was mine" sums up my present situation – and that of my long-suffering spouse, nine years ago.

We had "talked up" the idea of going to live in Spain full-time after we had bought a second home in a village set among the citrus groves of Valencia province. The location was but 20 minutes' drive from good beaches and a sizeable resort town, with mountain views from the first floor terrace.

The weather had been bad- so what's new? Record rainfall and consequent worsening of our 'rheumatics' – my left knee, his right shoulder and numerous other twinges. The climate is pronounced the best in Europe for arthritis and chest complaints and official figures state '300 days of sunshine each year'. What were we waiting for?

So, the second home would become our only home after selling up here in Hampshire, until we made a quantum leap to the next logical step – a larger house with garden and pool. In estate agents' speak, 'to live the dream'.

In our case, there had not been a long-held dream sustained through several years of annual holidays. No, we were hooked after just one visit – to Nerja on the Andalucian coast an hour's drive from Malaga airport. We fell for the ambience along with the food, the wine, the terracotta-roofed white houses decorated with colourful ceramic tiles and exotic flowering shrubs.

The two weeks over, we devoured books about our new enthusiasm – Gerald Brenan, Jan Morris, Ian Gibson's *Fire in the Blood* (fortuitously serialised on TV). And so, intrigued by the dramatic events of its turbulent history, fascinated by the architecture with its wrought iron tracery, seduced by the produce of the sun-drenched countryside, we fell under the potent spell of España.

Then plotting and planning began. At the time, we owned a house in Manchester, on the market for the past two years since we had moved back South from jobs in the 'cottonopolis'. As if by magic, within a month we had a buyer and therefore the wherewithal to buy a modest property in Spain.

What follows is a miscellany of anecdotes and notes, made during a six-year tenure of a second home in a village inland from the Valencian coast.

Buying The Car: A Renault Scenic With Left-Hand Drive

So, decision day had been and gone – now for the logistics of the whole thing. Up to now we had taken our Rover across to the Continent coping with driving on the right with a right-hand drive car, without too many hairy moments. But, facing the prospect of living in Spain all the time with constant exposure to Spaniards who mostly drive like matadors, the time was ripe for the purchase of a different steed.

I spotted the advert in one of the Sunday broadsheets – a company in Portsmouth who dealt solely in left-hand drive cars for people like us who were leaving their native shores -and so the process was set in motion. A phone call next day resulted in our visit to their office and an order placed for a Renault Megane. No, not the wobbly-bottom one! We were promised a delivery date six weeks hence, which was fine or I should say would have been fine, as the best laid plans did 'gang agley'. I shall explain.

The boss, a Mr Dearlove, agreed to take our faithful Rover from us if we could not sell it privately – a private sale could fetch a bit more than he would fork out as part-exchange for the new Renault. Quite nice to know – what we did not know was that would happen only when he found a buyer for the Rover.

Delay set in and our other plans were steaming ahead – sale of our house went through, the Spanish house neared building completion, we were selling off surplus furniture and other effects, taking unwanted goods and chattels to charity shops and the Sally Army and visiting relations and friends. Everything but the car! So, one thing we could not book was our car ferry crossing – this to be in June, when the middle-aged and childless migrated to France or Spain before the nightmare scenario of the school holidays. As Robert Benchley memorably remarked, there are two kinds of travel: first class and with children!

Mr Dearlove sat at his large desk, a man of middle years , dripping with fake gold – neck chain with bauble, wristwatch, numerous rings on his large, fleshy hands, perma-tan set off by a sky-blue open-necked shirt under a navy blazer with brass buttons.

He had the kind of looks to be found on race-tracks, behind and in front of bars and in casinos and other places of leisure and pleasure. He got to the point with a mixture of plausible chat and low cunning.

Delivery inexplicably affected by the Queen's Jubilee celebrations – in France? Pardon, madame? Surely some mistake? *Pour quoi?*

Mr Dearlove made frequent visits to his villa in Tenerife – topping up the perma-tan – and in his absence the office seemed to grind to a halt. Our telephone calls fell upon deaf ears or if not deaf suffered from selective hearing, employees were culled mainly from the Dearlove family – there was Kevin (there's always a Kevin), Julie and Mickey who did have blue eyes. Trouble was, they didn't know anything about our order. Inter-desk communication was zilch – until the return of Dearlove senior nothing would move, especially our car.

Her Majesty's Jubilee celebrations were indeed upon us, for 50 years on the throne. An undisputed excuse for the country to grind to a halt – but France too? We reserved our ferry berths for ourselves and our car. We were to sail from Portsmouth to Bilbao on 24 June, having been promised the house would be "ready any time after 20 June" and assuming that the car would materialise when the French had finished muscling in on our Jubilee celebrations!

In the event it fell to Big Al, not one of the family but a stalwart nonetheless, to sally forth to France and the Renault factory near Paris, to bring our new car over on a ferry, four days before our departure was to be. Knife-edge or what?

Big Al duly arrived complete with car – as ordered in a lovely shade of lime green and with steering wheel firmly on the left. Husband, a veteran of driving on the right side in the States and in Europe, nevertheless swallowed hard when he realised that 'this was it' – no going back. Practice was essential.

Because we were preparing our house for the removal of all our possessions, with the resulting Operation Clean-up, time was short. The new car stayed on the drive until the time came to vacate the house. So, it was that, after a snack lunch in the town, we could be spotted in the local lorry park (lorries absent on the road during the day), familiarising ourselves with the new vehicle. 'Ourselves' was a misnomer – I, shattered by events beyond my control, left it to my other half. The boy done well and we arrived at the ferry port safely after all. It would be easier the other side of the Bay of Biscay!

We're Off!

The day came when we had to empty the house we had called home for nine years, not a long time but long enough to accumulate plenty of stuff. So, the stuff was staring us in the face- asking "What is to be done with us things?"

The large items- beds, sofas, chairs, and tables- would be packed expertly by the removal men. We had undertaken to pack clothes, linen, books, tapes, records, cushions, glass, china, pictures and ornaments – all the awkward things.

First of all we had to acquire boxes, cardboard for the use of. The local supermarkets came up with some and the removal men supplied the rest. As with all activities, there is a right way and a wrong way. A boxful of books, 'wrong' – too heavy for even the brawniest to lift. 'Right' -books at bottom, then make up with bulky but light items, e.g. pillows, cushions, duvets, padded anoraks, etc. etc. Common sense really! Surprisingly, folded sheets are comparatively heavy. Must be something to do with physics (not my strongest school subject)...

Packing done, now the pushing and heaving – into one area ready for removal men, who ruled the roost regarding the 'modus operandi'. Everything must be made as easy as absolutely possible for these masters of their universe.

Decisions, decisions ... should we opt for a short crossing e.g. Portsmouth to Caen or Cherbourg, then a long drive down through France and thence to Spain's Costa Blanca? Or, take the Portsmouth to Bilbao 30-hour crossing and drive across Spain bypassing Burgos, Zaragoza and over-nighting in Teruel? This would leave a two and a half hour drive next morning. As at that time we were more familiar with road trips in France we decided on Caen.

Disembarking from the 'Pride of Normandie' at 3.30 pm, we had several hours of daylight driving before we needed to find somewhere to rest our heads. Midsummer meant a long, light evening, but hunger and fatigue dictated our stopping at 6 o'clock when we found a small, friendly hotel in an attractive little town on the banks of a river.

A couple of glasses of red wine, a delicious omelette with frites and a stroll around by the river restored our faith in human nature and led to a quiet and peaceful night's sleep. Then came the dawn and the need to press on toward our destination- no time for lingering in the pleasant square with its church, three cafés and fruit and vegetable market already open at eight o'clock. No, we must not succumb to pavement people - watching. It was time to go.

Driving in France can be delightful but also it can be rather boring. Away from Normandy and Brittany the long roads in the south-west of the country stretch for kilometre after kilometre of flat, rural acres. Clumps of trees stand sentinel along the way, the ubiquitous poplar acting as windbreaks for the farmers.

Small towns along the way varied in their provision of refreshment. But what did not vary was the rigid timing of luncheon. We were enlightened in this respect when we arrived at 1.45 pm on the doorstep of a charming bistro, only to be turned away as 'too late'.

To us, confirmed Hispanophiles, this behaviour was odd indeed. The Spanish lunch 'hour' tends to begin late, never before one o'clock- and can last until at least 3.30 pm and more often 4. This does have a downside in that the evening dinner times are also late, with Spaniards sallying forth to eat at around 9 o'clock. Some restaurants do not even open for business until 8.

But this was France and it was to French customs we must perforce become accustomed during our three days in the country. Fortunately we had an emergency packet of biscuits plus apples and a bar of chocolate. This had to suffice until our evening port of call.

We turned off the autoroute to a large village boasting a *chambre d 'hote* and two B&Bs. A room for the night was to be had in one of the B & Bs, but no evening meal was on offer. Luckily, the '*d'hote*' had a bar-restaurant, to which we repaired for an excellent supper at the civilised hour of seven o'clock. But, a fly in the ointment awaited us.

After a stroll around the village and a glass of beer at the bar we laid our heads down at about 10 o'clock and were soon in the Land of Nod. Our slumbers were disturbed three hours later by very interesting 'noises' coming from the next room.

A creaking bed featured heavily, accompanied by what could be described as screaming, reminiscent of the tennis player Maria Sharapova on an especially bad day. It did stop – exhaustion? – only to be resumed with the coming of the dawn and apparently their second wind! We assumed the enthusiasm to be attributed to possibly their newly-wed status or an exciting, perhaps illicit, liaison made more delightful by their being in the land of *l 'amour, la belle France*. Who knows? We named them 'The Screaming Bonkers' and left after breakfast to resume our odyssey.

Our journey from Hampshire to the Alta Marina district of the Valenciana province became familiar and was not usually eventful in the Ranulph Fiennes-type of eventful. But, it was fraught with happenings, some of them bizarre.

There was the small hotel in Central France where the only room available was next to the kitchen – a kitchen open all hours into the small ones, well, one a.m. anyway. Tired from driving in the unrelenting heat we longed for sleep. The Gallic Gordon Ramsay next door had other ideas. With his '*Mon Dieus*' '*Sacre Bleus*' and worse, he ruled the place with a rod of invective, loud at that. His staff were either thick or insubordinate or both, for they could not seem to do anything right.

But, the fare that emerged from his domain was delicious. For supper we had been served with the best mushroom omelettes ever, with warm crusty rolls and a carafe of Burgundy. Coffee at breakfast was excellent and again the bread was to die for, with pale yellow butter and homemade cherry jam.

So, we forgave the noise, paid the bill and drove on to the next sojourn, never booked ahead so keeping the constant state of surprise!

To Go Or To Stay?

And so from the wheels to the roof over our heads, or rather rooves as not content with buying one abode we were set on course for buying another. Things were not going to be simple, though. House number one was to be ready for us in June '02, but as we had decided to move to Spain on a permanent basis we thought something a little larger plus a pool for those long, hot summers would be desirable.

January '02 found us in Denia, spending a fortnight in a hotel during which we would inspect the building of our future home. One of the attractions laid on for the clientele was a visit from an estate agent, Gerry by name. His sales pitch was not aggressive, rather 'take it or leave it' seemed to be his motto. Maybe this was the appeal – at any rate a few days later we were inspecting a site on the outskirts of the town. A house with views of the sea and of the local mountain was to be built here, as soon as a buyer came along.

To cut it short, we went for it! We bought the land two months later and put the unfinished house in the village up for sale. One of the hotel staff put in a bid for it, but withdrew after she split up with her boyfriend. No other offers came up by the time we were ready to depart the UK, so, having sold our house in Hampshire, we decided to live in the first dwelling until the second was built – to take one year.

People say when you buy abroad you 'leave your brains behind'- a bit harsh, but we must have been rather foolish. Because, although we had the money from the UK sale to buy the house and have some 'change' left, we did not foresee one essential point – what if we found we did not after all want to be full-time residents? Of course, this is exactly what happened! I, with two years' worth of Spanish lessons under my belt, could have stayed on, but the other half of the partnership declared:" No, sorry, but I can't do this! I must have a place in the UK."

And so, after four months, we made plans to travel to our old stamping-ground to find a small house, with the intention of keeping the village house on as a second home (the original idea). Ergo, we would not be able to proceed with the purchase of the second house. But, we had to comply with the builder's needs for money to carry on. Payment of two thirds of the costs must be found, to be repaid when someone wanted to buy the embryo house.

There was nothing for it but to bite the bullet and pay up, mercifully in instalments. Builder Klaus was confident that a buyer would be found as soon as the roof stage was reached, giving a whole new meaning to the phrase 'a roof over one's head'. But, the roof was put on, windows and doors went in, in short the house that Klaus built was finished, only to wait for a buyer until more than a year later.

He did emerge at the end of 2003, with his wife, to take over the now completed dwelling, all set to sign up in mid-February 2004. But, what's this? A spanner in the works! The developer must put in a sewer. The Montgo national park must have proper facilities and the septic tanks were relegated to the past, a blessed memory. The 21st century had arrived and with it modernity.

The drains, my dear, and the people! Klaus, Denia's mayor, the architect, the notary – all these characters met to discuss the iniquity of the new policy.

The months passed. We returned to the UK in late March '04, leaving the drains to be made, the buyers in limbo and in thrall to their London-based lawyers – to become legendary for bringing a whole new meaning to "dotting the 'i's and crossing the 't's".

We went to the States in April, visiting the Big Easy or N'Awlins and touring South Louisiana and part of Mississippi. It was a fascinating journey and took our minds far away from Spain and its drains. Husband saw Vicksburg, siege bound in the Civil War – and I heard the jazz in Bourbon Street, New Orleans, a long-held dream.

But there was no permanent escape and in June we returned to Benivergel and the crane and the bulldozer – icons of modern Spain. In China cranes bring good fortune, in Russia they are regarded as special birds, but in Spain they bring building ad infinitum and subsequent millions of euros. No real progress had been made in Denia and the buyers were still hanging on in there. We left on 21 July to take on the management of grandkids until 8 September, when they returned to their schools and we returned once more to Spain.

It would be a whole year before we recouped the money we had paid over and by then we were becoming very disenchanted with things Spanish. Time to move on?

Playing Marbles

When we bought the then unfinished house in October 2001 we were told firmly that the marble workshop directly opposite would be closing down and moving to a site on the *poligono industrial* (industrial estate), SOON. Being fully aware of the *'mañana'* tendency, we asked: "What does 'soon' mean? In a few weeks, months? Next year, maybe?" Agent Alex settled for 'next year'.

It would be a full four years before any sign of departure were to happen – December 2005 saw the removal of several large slabs of marble. Up until that point replenishment had been the norm.

So, fast forward a couple of months to see, parked outside our house, a lorry with crane attached, lifting ready-to-use slabs from the yard to the interior of the lorry. *MUY BIEN*! But, read on…one day enthusiasm overtook common sense and the lorry's chassis began to slide. Consternation! Jose and Miguel plus two other helpers rushed to prop up the vehicle with whatever they could lay their hands on.

I summoned up my Spanish vocabulary and asked Jose the manager: "*Cuando ve usted hasta el poligono industrial?*" His reply: "*Proxima semana*". But that was last week and no action has taken place since then. Three hours of this activity and we needed to move our car from our parking space in front of the house to the road. Said lorry had perforce to budge up. Next day, more of the same – and for the whole week.

By March, when we had returned for a month, the firm had actually left. That is to say, the workers plus most of the marble and the tools of the trade, while leaving behind the large and unlovely metal gantries overhead) the yard, the rusty old gate and the creaking ancient doors. It was to be a further year before something happened on the site, in

February 2007. The 'something' was a nasty shock- a block of 26 apartments to be erected, with underground car park, necessitating a fairly massive excavation project.

"Por favor, marmoles, volver!"

The Noise, My Dear – And The People!

We found out very early on in our sojourns in Benivergel that it was no place for getting eight hours' sleep at night. Sometimes, even managing to sleep at all was well nigh impossible.

The Spanish people have a well-deserved reputation for being the noisiest in Europe and their animals must be up there too.

An assortment of dogs in the village would start a cacophony just as we had laid down our heads at say, 11 o'clock. We knew some by sight – the snappy Scottie, the growly Alsatian and the (apparently) unfed Rottweiler. They could be heard often during the day also, but it was the nocturnal din that bothered us the most.

Then there were the early mornings. Despite 'rules' from the *ayuntamiento* decreeing there should be no loud noise before eight a.m., the marble workshop opened for business at least 20 minutes before that. On went the radio, blaring forth pop songs and the frenetic shouting of excitable presenters, together with the inevitable sawing and cutting of the hardest material known to man.

Then there was the garbage truck, making its rounds in the early hours. We sometimes slept through it, but not often. Three times a week, at any time after three a.m. the communal *basura* bin was emptied. Crash, bang, wallop – accompanied by the driver's radio. Earplugs became the order of the night!

Spaniards love fireworks, not just on high days and holidays but at any excuse to celebrate. Birthdays, weddings, football matches – out came the rockets and squibs. With wild abandon they were set off at all hours – yet another source of noise! The loudest we ever heard were the excruciating *mascletas*, let off at two o'clock daily for the week of the Valencian Fallas (described elsewhere). These not only banged but smoked – a truly appalling combination for those of a nervous disposition.

But, back to the village and before that let us visit the nearest town, Ondara.

On the day before festivities began, to last ten days, we went to buy groceries in the supermarket. We were astonished to see what struck us as an indiscriminate use of 'firepower' strung out between trees and posts, to be lit from boxes. Conflagrations were planned in no uncertain terms. Dangerous or what?

When the Benivergel team wins a match or even a striker scores a goal, off go the rockets. Similarly, Paco the once-upon-a-time bullfighter is 75 – what better reason for more of the same to be set off?

The Hustlers

We walk towards the carousel at Alicante airport and towards our little house among the orange groves, eight hours door-to-door from our UK base in Hampshire. All's well, but what's this? Realtors hustling for business in the *aeropuerto*, a new tactic!

Asserting:" We have a place in Spain already" deterred the first two, but the third was either more brass-necked or more desperate, the rictus smile unfaltering as she countered with "We are promoting the concept of re-locating in Spain"...

That was clear enough i.e. (a) if you regretted the purchase made on a spur-of-the- moment "no obligation" inspection trip or (b) find you have on each side neighbours from hell or (c) the property you bought with your hard-earned wherewithal is too small/too big/infested with cockroaches/mosquitoes/flies, or as the King of Siam memorably stated "etcetera, etcetera, ETCETERA", well, hey – sell it and buy something better from us!

One of these hopeful hustlers stopping to chat up arrivals from Gatwick was even touting as an incentive a new Ford Fiesta – though his colleague didn't seem quite certain about this. Perhaps they had not attended the same sales pitch meeting!

Probably one inescapable fact emerges from this situation, namely this: there is an abundance of property on the market, being chased by too many sellers and not enough buyers. Is the bubble finally about to burst?

With such a vast preponderance of property *'Se Vende'* along the Costa Blanca and in *'el campo'* too the thought occurs: "Who is going to buy each and every one of these villas/apartments/fincas?"

A favourite adage uttered by realtors is that for each dwelling there is an ideal buyer – that desirable being just has to be found! Mature readers of the Sunday Times may recall the doyen of estate agents, Roy Brooks, and his idiosyncratic classified ads. His advertising prose was deep purple and imbued with a blistering honesty. For Roy a bathroom was not compact, it was 'miniscule', a master bedroom did not have "an attractive urban roofscape view" – it overlooked a derelict iron foundry. "Some renovation with TLC needed" became "in an advanced state of neglect, crying out for a DIY buff with loads of money and a fertile imagination to turn this ruin into a desirable residence".

If this theory holds water, does it mean that the rumoured number of 800,000 German retirees, hell-bent for Spain clutching their wads of euros, will answer the equivalent number of 'targeted ads'? I think we should be told!

Flamenco ...Or Not So Much?

Is it flamenco, do you think?

A few years ago, back in the day of my weekly Spanish lessons, our tutor Pilar from Valencia explained to us that the true, authentic flamenco sound was in song and not so much in dance.

The gypsies of Andalusia – the Al-Andalus of the Moors – sang about their hard and savage lives, said Elena. "It is heartfelt because they sing the truth."

So, was the workman Miguel giving us a free performance of something special, something tourists would fork out many euros to hear? Anything is possible. But, I am sure my forthright mother would have something pithy to utter - something like:" My cat sounds better than that when she's arguing with one of her admirers, under my window!"

Miguel was employed by the chief local builder, one Vicente Sanchez or *'el jefe'*, to carry out a variety of tasks. On this particular day he was transporting rubble from one site to another, in a large wheelbarrow. As he staggered along he gave voice – I won't call it singing – very loudly and not melodiously! The sound was a cross between Chinese opera and a raucous cat. But, perhaps this was the true flamenco?

As the time was not yet seven-thirty and we had not yet had our early morning tea, we were not about to ask him. Besides, we did not want in any way to encourage him, any more than Maggie Smith's character wanted Ivor Novello at the piano in 'Gosford Park'.

Give Me A Break!

When are we going to have a pavement/sidewalk (our Town Hall secretary has a Hockney print on his office wall, is very pro-Californian and uses Americanisms in his day-to-day conversation) is our and three neighbours' plea? After two months we were still trudging through loose earth and gravel-and trudging lumps of the same into our smart new homes. We were also still awaiting 'the boys from the blackstuff' and a road surface!

One wonderful day the pavement/sidewalk was laid – oh joy! And, with the imminent arrival of our daughter and family in a hire car from Alicante airport, Peter scoured the site for suitable pieces of brick and cement from which he built a ramp abutting the newly-laid kerb, to make it easier to drive the car into our designated car space at front of the house.

This was a first, as for eight weeks we had been parking the car 200 metres away in a side road. So, as a dutiful spouse I leapt up and out of the front door to wave him in. But, fate deemed otherwise. I'd forgotten to buckle my shoes, tripped on the step and fell, my left leg buckling under me. Within seconds a bump appeared on the ankle bone.

Consternation set in – husband jumped from car, halfway into the patio and helped me to a chair. We packed the injury with ice cubes and elevated the limb as all good first aiders do – and went straight into denial. "No, it's not broken, just a sprain." This despite a faint memory of daughter two's fractured arm and its protuberance thereon. I hobbled around the house, upstairs and downstairs, for three days with the affected area turning all colours of the rainbow. Oddly though with not a lot of pain – no sense, no feeling?

When daughter one (a nurse) arrived she pronounced the ankle broken: It's off to hospital for you, Mother!" So, off we went to spend three hours in Denia hospital returning at 7 pm with my left leg in plaster up to the knee – a white sock!

The Ash Grove

We had been in our house on the edge of a large orange grove for a couple of weeks. The days had not been peaceful, on account of a terrace conversion a few doors down. Spanish workmen rise early, before sun-up sometimes, and these two were no exception. So, 7.30 am brought banging, tapping, drilling and worst of all raising buckets by a rickety, squeaky old pulley that had seen far better days. All this activity was accompanied by shouting, in a dialect that bore no relation to the Castilian Spanish of my lessons or the local Valenciano.

Anyway, to another annoyance – I looked out of the window at about 8 am to see, borne on the mistral type breeze, fragments of ash, settling on the newly-washed car, the garden furniture, pot plants and every other surface. Consternation! Where was the fire?

Not wishing to emulate the citizens of Pompeii, we ran outside to investigate. The ash seemed to be floating over the orange grove but we could not discern any form of human presence. The village copper was at the end of the road answering a complaint from the man who was building a house on the site formerly a rubbish dump. I accosted him, whereupon he pointed to his watch and said "*Once, Once*" and rushed off. Did he have an appointment at 11 am or what?

We returned to the oranges, plunged into the trees and found the culprits, a young Spaniard who spoke some English and an older one who did not. I spoke to them in my halting Spanish and my husband in sign language, letting them know we were not best pleased.

All was revealed. The elder man, who sported headgear reminiscent of Beau Geste with a dash of such worn by beekeepers, produced a sheaf of papers from the Town Hall: his permit to burn surplus branches for two days from seven until 11 am. Well, at least we knew what was going on and that we had to suffer another ash-filled morning before we could embark on Operation Clean-up. Those quaint Spanish customs – they're wonderful!

Places In The Sun – The Way They Were!

Our 'place in the sun' is one of 10 townhouses on the edge of a small Spanish town, built in the style of the older properties in its *Calle Mayor* and the other *calles* , but with modern features at which the locals marvel.

We have three bedrooms and two bathrooms, a spacious living-room and roomy kitchen, roof terrace and courtyards front and back, with the traditional small balcony for pot plants at front. All windows and sliding glazed doors are fitted with mosquito nets and *persianas*.

Views are great – orange groves and mountains surround us and we are but 15 minutes' drive from the coast and good beaches. We are a few minutes' walk from no less than seven bars, most serving lunches (*menu del dia*) at reasonable prices.

But, this is not enough for some folk – those among us who have moved from grander abodes, detached villas with large plots given over to landscaped gardens, pools, outside kitchens and all the other paraphernalia of 'the good life'.

No, they must start adding on things – *nayas*, loggias, conservatories, huge sliding canopies (why buy a south-facing plot if you don't want a lot of sun?!?) and even converting roof terraces into bedrooms.

What began as a neat modest development has become a hotch-potch and, quite frankly, some additions are downright eyesores. Anything goes, it seems – whatever you want you can have, at no matter what inconvenience to your neighbour. Wreck his view, host noisy gatherings in your tailor-made 'alfresco' entertainment area – just make merry at all costs!

Back in the Land of UK, where life-style programmes dominate the television screens, it is not surprising if a very large proportion of the citizenry descends on the DIY stores at weekends. They fill their cars with timber, wallpaper, paint and other necessities of their home improvement projects.

Winston Churchill once remarked that advertising was A GOOD THING because it encouraged the lower classes to aspire to a better life – this was to suppose they had access to more spending power to match their aspirations! Lord Leverhulme, on the other side of the equation, said "I know that half of what I spend on advertising (on soap and washing powder) is wasted. Trouble is, I don't know which half!"

There are two points here, surely? Folk who reside in the UK, with its long, cold, wet winters and unpredictable summers, need to make their homes as attractive as they can reasonably afford – both time and money-wise. After all they are in them most of the time! But here, in sunny Spain? I thought that one of the main advantages in living under the Spanish sun was to be able to leave behind all that DIY and lawn mowing, embracing the benefits extolled by estate agents from Barcelona to Malaga and beyond. What is the phrase? *Vivir el sueno*, I think. *Salud!*

Cutting Edge Science Valenciano Style

Time to turn to Valencia, Spain's third city and home to, it claims, the largest cultural leisure complex in Europe. This is- *La Ciutat de les arts y les sciences*, on the *'Avenida Antipista del Saler'*, a 'bus ride from the rail station in the centre of the city'. We were too early for the unfinished *Palacio de las Artes* when we arrived one day in 2002 and for the largest marine park, which was to rival Sea World in Florida with its underwater voyage and promise of 'knowing the life beneath the waves'.

The Science Museum was complete, though, with its Foucault's pendulum one of the main attractions and so was *L'Hemisferic*, an amazing building in the shape of the human eye, encompassing three audiovisual shows – Planetarium, Laserium and IMAX. A bonus is personalised narration in English.

The Foucault's pendulum, showing the rotation of the earth and so named after its inventor French physicist Leon Foucault, was first exhibited to the public in 1851 in the Paris Observatory and thence to the dome of the Pantheon. Unfortunately in 2010 it was damaged beyond repair. But, a replica had been made in 1995 and it is this one that can be seen to this day in the Pantheon, after a number of years in the Musee des Arts et Metiers.

The City of Arts and Sciences was built at the end of the former riverbed of the river Turia, which after a catastrophic flood was drained and rerouted in 1957. Its centrepiece, *L'Hemisferic* or the planetarium, opened in 1998 to an astonished public. It resembles a giant eye, with opening eyelid that opens to access the water pool. An aluminum shutter folds upward to form a brise-soleil roof that opens to reveal the dome, the eye's pupil – the Ominax theatre.

Another amazing and novel structure is the Science Museum – it resembles the skeleton of a whale and is 220 metres long by 80 metres wide. About two-thirds of this space is devoted to exhibitions, including the 'Chromosome Forest', showing the sequencing of human DNA.

The open-air oceanographic park is the largest in Europe at 110,000 square metres and containing 42 million litres of water. Another unusual design, it is built in the shape of a water lily by architect Felix Candela. Each building represents different aquatic environments including the Mediterranean, Wetlands, Temperate and Tropical Seas, Oceans, the Antarctic, the Arctic and the Red Sea. More than 500 species dwell here, including dolphins, belugas, walruses, sea lions, seals, penguins, turtles, sharks and rays, besides wetland bird species.

The last component to open, in 2005, El Palau de les Arts Reina Sofia – a tribute to the Queen of Spain – is dedicated to music and the scenic arts. Again, it is an impressive edifice and is surrounded by 87,000 square metres of water and landscape. It has become the Valencia Opera House. Imaginatively conceived and not without controversy, brilliantly executed and well received, the 'city' is the most important tourist destination in Valencia.

It's Fiesta Time!

In Valencia – and in Denia, Oliva and Pego in the Marina Alta region – each year on 17 March Las Fallas are held. Gigantic papier-mâché figures are built by the numerous districts, in the style of television's Spitting Image – depicting politicians, media celebrities and show-biz personalities.

Captions in the Valencian dialect are barbed and irreverent with world statesmen and women mercifully mocked, from Maggie Thatcher (still deemed a VIP in Europe) to George W. Bush and Condoleezza Rice. Spaniards, since the decline of *machismo* in their country and the rise of the matriarchal society, respect strong women.

Towns and villages inland and on the Costa Blanca, in common with other Spanish settlements stage enthusiastic and interminable *fiestas*. In Ondara, for several summer months one celebration merges into another. Saints' days, *Los Moros y Los Cristianos* (the commemoration of the expulsion of the Moors in the 15th century after 700 years' occupation) and for local reasons. One of the latter category in a nearby coastal town is The Burial of the Sardine.

Back to the *fallas* – fires – these need a little explanation. The tradition in early spring many years ago was for the carpenters – in honour of their patron saint Joseph – to set fire to their left-over pieces of timber and other pieces of surplus material. This ceremony evolved into the famous spectacle of today, with processions of elaborately dressed and coiffed women, marching bands representing artisans' guilds and others, and of course plenty of fireworks – including the ear-splitting *mascletas*. These smoky 'bangers' are set off at two o'clock every day for a week. No comment!

Fiestas – Do They Need Them?

The first time I remember hearing the word *'fiesta'* was as the title of a novel by Ernest Hemingway, a noted *aficionado* of the bullfight and the San Fermin bull-running spectacle in Pamplona.

The book featured one Lady Brett Ashley and assorted Brit Hispanophiles as they followed the bullfights and festivals throughout much of Spain. Many years have passed since I read it and now I have first-hand experience of many *fiestas* – The Valencian Fallas, Barcelona's Carnaval, Semana Santa (Easter Week) in Seville …and the week-long village celebrations of Saints' days, besides 'jollies' of varying length held in the clustered villages and small towns in the Marina Alta region.

In Ondara, our nearest town, the legend *'Bones Festes'* strung across the main street is left suspended all summer – they have three fiestas and it is just not worth taking it down until they are all over!

It amazes us that the tradition of these parties is carried on in this modern era, when every Spaniard seems to own a car – or at least a white van – meaning mobility far beyond the imagination of their parents, almost every house has a television aerial and mobile phones are attached to most persons between 12 and 40. Travel agents – there are four in Denia – advertising the charms of faraway places with strange-sounding names, achieve good results. Spaniards have shed their reputation for insularity and go abroad as they are exhorted to.

Ergo, do they need *fiestas*? Except for the big cities where massive amounts of euros are splashed out on ever-more spectacular sights and where tourists abound, many taking their annual vacations so as to catch the carnivals, I do wonder if the villagers would miss them so very much.

A Load Of Old (And Clever) Bull

One of Denia's summer programme events and a must-see, if only once, is *'Las Bous en la Mar'*. In Castiliano they would be *Las Toros* but in Valenciano *Las Bous*, the bulls, who for two weeks are released from pens and let through barriers on the main street, *Calle Marques de Campo*, to thunder down to the quayside.

Reaching this point, they are corralled into another pen, whence they are released at intervals to the noisy taunting of the local lads. These testosterone-filled adolescents stripped to their waists and strutting their stuff, go about their business. This has the sole aim of pushing the bulls into the sea.

Water is not the natural habitat of these noble animals and they are not best pleased at this summary treatment. But, what's this? Retribution lies waiting in the wings, in the vengeful shape of three mature bulls – wily enough to turn the tables and push their tormentors into the water. *Jovenes en la mar!*

More Bull – Village-Style

Most serious Hispanophiles have heard of the running of the bulls festival in Pamplona – the San Fermin beloved of Ernest Hemingway in his action-packed heyday. This ancient ritual is celebrated also in small towns throughout Spain with just as much enthusiasm.

'Our' village-into-town is no exception. After Denia's festivities, in August, the Mayor and his council swing into action. Wooden structures are erected along the main streets – *Calle Mayor* and others, and the *Plaza del Ayuntamiento*. The large new car park is covered with sand ready for the arrival of the running bulls. This is where they strut their stuff for the delectation of the watching populace plus visitors from the surrounding villages and tourists who happened to be in the area.

The seven bars – yes, seven! – do a roaring trade in wines and beers, but there is little or no accompanying drunkenness or loutish behaviour. Although noisy people, Spaniards rarely become ugly or nasty after drink taken. What is it with the Anglo-Saxon – is it something atavistic from our distant past, an unfortunate inheritance from our rough ancestors?

In Veno Veritas

Any comments about life in Spain would be incomplete without some reference to its wine, second to none in our opinion. From the northwest region of Galicia to Jerez – home of sherry – the country has about three million acres planted with vines, making it the most widely planted wine-producing nation in the world.

However, France and Italy both produce more wine. This is due to wide spacing of very old vines and dry soil found in many Spanish wine regions. From 400 varieties of native grape only 20 of these provide 80 per cent of the production- including Tempranillo, Albarino, Carinena and Monastrell.

Archaeologists believe that grapes were first cultivated at least as long ago as 3000 BC, before the Phoenicians founded their trading post of Cadiz around 1100 BC. Later, the Carthaginians and then the Roman conquerors developed the viticulture of the country and exporting and trading throughout the Roman Empire began and flourished. The Romans seem to have developed a taste for Spanish wines above their native Italian ones – amphorae have been found in ruins of Roman settlements in Normandy, the Loire Valley and Provence. Roman soldiers in Britain and Germany were kept supplied too!

The prolific writer Pliny the Elder praised the wine from Tarragona while Ovid commented that one known as Saguntum was good only for getting your mistress drunk!

After the 700-year Moorish occupation of Spain the *Reconquista* began exporting wines, with Bilbao a large port trading with Bristol, London and Southampton. In 1492, when 'Columbus sailed the ocean blue', the

New World became a new export market and offered a new wine-producing area.

As exports to England waned after Henry VIII's divorce from Catherine of Aragon and Spanish debt increased after the Spanish Armada, Philip II depended on the income from his colonies. By the end of the 19th century sparkling wine in the shape of Cava had emerged in Catalonia, rivalling the Champagne region in worldwide production.

The Civil War and the Second World War hit the wine markets in different ways, but by the 1960s sherry was again popular and Rioja wine was in demand. Fast-forward to 1986 with Spain's entry into the European Union and economic aid to the rural wine industries of Galicia and La Mancha. The dawn of the 21st century saw Spain enjoying a reputation as a serious competitor in the world wine market. From someone who had thought French wines reigned supreme and Italian close second, Spanish wines were a revelation. Whenever we were lucky enough to come upon a wine-tasting or a local fiesta, we took part with gusto. Our favourite place, one at which we broke our journey three times for B & B, was Carinena, a small town in Aragon with several *bodegas* and a wonderful wine museum. The local red is to die for and has its own denomination from the local grape, Carinena.

I can say with all honesty that even in the humblest of restaurants we never had an inferior wine. Settling for 'the house' was always fine.

Vale Of Plenty

Olives, lemons, almonds – fruits of the soil in the land of plenty that is the Jalon Valley. It was along the road that winds through this productive vale that we would drive, on most Saturday mornings during our stays in our Spanish house.

The attraction was the weekly '*rastro*' a huge flea market beginning on the area of ground underneath the road bridge into the town and ending about 500 metres away, opposite a new row of shops and cafes.

The first stop was the car park, a rough, grassy patch with a few old trees dotted around. This enterprise was run by a man and his daughter, charging one euro per car, no time limit. The man's wife was stationed by the entrance at the side of the road, selling five-kilo bags of oranges at five euros each bag.

Across the bridge and into the melee of stalls and throngs of people from the surrounding villages and hamlets – locals and tourists alike flocked to the magnet of the *rastro* and also the Xalo wine co-operative on the opposite side of the busy main road. In this temple to the grape we would each help ourselves to a tiny plastic cup and sip taste-size quantities of the wines on offer for our delectation. In this way we would become nicely relaxed without in any way intoxicated, just the right mood in which to wander the flea market.

Clothes, shoes, jewellery, bags, books and pictures, plants – all there, besides other stalls beloved of the true *aficionado* of rastros. These were the ones displaying objects often rudely called 'junk', the ones whose perusal could occasionally yield something special – 'a real find'. It was, of course, this encouraging possibility that kept the faithful returning time after time – Saturday after Saturday – in the fervent hope that on one of those times a Clarice Cliff teapot or a Susie Cooper bowl would be lurking underneath the dross.

Another curiosity along the way is the Hallelujah Bar, run by an enterprising Spaniard of uncertain age with a histrionic flair. He had a nice line in impromptu entertainment. When there was a number of customers in the bar, say about 20 of us, he would hold aloft a drinking vessel especial to Spain, a bulbous glass container with a long spout filled with wine. Then came the party trick...he would tilt the vessel about two feet above his upturned face so that the wine would trickle into his mouth with no spillage. This is more difficult than it sounds! To show our appreciation we would shout 'Hallelujah!!

The bar sold not only wine and beer plus spirits, as did other bars, but novelties such as glass slippers filled with brandy, carved boxes filled with sugared almonds, numerous odd-shaped bottles and flagons and not to forget large bags of oranges and lemons. There was also seating outside, under a huge old olive tree – augmented with big parasols over tables providing shade from the wall-to-wall sunshine, habitual in this area of Spain from May to October.

Another attraction in the town was the wine museum. Short on publicity and difficult to find, this ancient building was hidden away several metres from a side street off the road to the next village. It was worth the search, though – a small but fascinating collection of wine memorabilia together with the history of viticulture in the valley, explained by a charming and knowledgeable guide. She told us that her family had owned the house in which the museum was kept and had been one of the chief producers of *vino tinto*, supplying the co-operative where we had been tasting the wares earlier. She showed us their original *bodegon* (cellar), no longer in use, but redolent of past tastings – and sales too.

So, even if your purchases in the *rastro* amounted to no more than a bag of liquorice, a couple of second-hand books and your refreshment no more than cups of coffee or hot chocolate, it was pretty easy to while away a few hours on a Saturday. *Salud*!

A Community Of Compassion

One of the unusual sights to see in the Marina Alta region is the former leper hospital at Fontilles. About eight winding kilometres from the small town of Orba, the village is perched above the Luguar valley, looking across to the Sierra del Migdia.

Here the air is crystal clear – bliss on a hot and humid day – and the vegetation lush and varied. There is one bar doubling as a small general store, but the surprise attraction is a theatre – hardly the National but which nonetheless proudly presents a monthly production for several days in the summer months.

On the day we visited, in May, the actors seemed to be 'resting' as no poster was evident with news of anything in the near future. We had a glass of San Miguel in the bar and asked if they knew anything, but answer came there none: "*No se, perdon*".

More than a century ago in 1902 a Jesuit priest, Father Carlos and a lawyer, Don Joaquin Ballester, determined to open a sanatorium to care for leprosy patients. Several years later the Saint Francisco de Borja opened its doors to patients from all over Spain and by 1909 Fontilles had become a village.

In that year the first eight patients entered the hospital, attended by the sisters *Franciscanas de la Immaculada* and the Jesuits of the *Compania de Jesus*, who have continued through the years with this work. It is staffed also by volunteers and of course by medical and specialist doctors. As a village it has its own facilities: bakery, carpenter, smithy, printing house, shoemaker, hairdresser and gardener.

In 1947 Fontilles became a training centre for experts from around the world with every year about 70 doctors and others being taught how to combat leprosy. Now world-famous, Fontilles continues its work today, with 80 in-patients and 150 out-patients. Financing comes from the Spanish public health service and from private charity too.

The future of this remarkable institution is hopeful. Besides caring for the remaining leprosy sufferers, a new era has begun of helping socially abandoned individuals who have been left with chronic diseases and no pensions. Assistance comes from the Generalitat Valencia and the Society of Jesus.

They Can Take That Away From Me

Readers may know of LRAU (the by now famous/infamous Valencian land law that allows developers to appropriate portions of house-owners' acreage and then charge them for infrastructure which they do not want or need). "They can't take that away from me" – or can they?

Example: a British couple had sold their property in Kent and bought a rural house with a small (1,000 square-metres) orchard, mainly lemon trees. One month after moving in they were informed by a neighbour that the area was earmarked for a LRAU development. The effect was that they should give up half their land – to be compensated for 250 square metres, thus ceding one-quarter in payment for infrastructure for the planned industrial estate. Rough justice?

On the edge of a small town in a small house, one of a terrace of 10 with courtyards front and back, we are in no danger from such legal action. However, we have other challenges. At the back of the L-shaped development was an old olive grove. What was going to happen to this? We asked the builder/estate agent. There were then no firm plans. Could be for visitors' car parking, possibly a swimming pool if enough owners wanted one – fate undecided.

Eventually, with euros on their eyeballs, the firm made two decisions. First, they sold the house they had kept as a company asset for use by their own (English) family members; second, they offered the olive grove in strips to the owners whose boundary walls abutted the ground. Chaos ensued – some wanted to buy, others dithered and two refused point-blank. The end result was for two people to buy the whole lot between them – three strips each.

The past year or so has seen a welter of indiscriminate building – ground floor extension and bedrooms on his upper terrace by one of the two, plus an enormous 'carport'/embryo garage on his extra land; conversion of terrace into rooms and numerous interior (noisy) alterations to the former company house and yet a third terrace conversion – by the slowest workers in Spain – plus another 'carport'. The quote marks are because a well-known practice is for such a modest construction to be put up, left a few years then turn it into something more solid – a full-blown garage!

There seems no such thing as planning and certainly no regard paid to aesthetic considerations – such a travesty of the attractive look of the original terrace. From our viewpoint we say with feeling: "A plague on all your houses!"

Highway Robbery

I can see him now, leaping from his little red car to stand in front of our car, giving us instructions – chief of these was to place the warning triangle 30 metres down the highway behind the stationary car.

It went like this: we had stopped for a *cafe con leche* at a roadside service station, parking the locked car under a bamboo canopy along with a number of others. Suitably refreshed, we resumed our journey along the fairly quiet, Sunday afternoon *autovia* towards our overnight stop, Zarautz on the coast, a strategic point before driving to the French border, to cross it at Irun. Should have been uneventful but, the best laid schemes of mice and men…

Suddenly all was not well with the car. We felt a jolt to the right and then we were lurching along on three tyres. The back one on the passenger side had burst! Consternation – the car was just one year old. Shocking or what?

And so it was that I dealt with the triangle while my husband examined the back tyre on the passenger side, neither of us watching the 'helpful' young man. This was a mistake, but bear in mind we were in a state of shock. We looked up to see the red car about 100 metres on its way. "Oh, well, I expect he's on his way to a family gathering," I remarked, remembering the usual custom on Sundays.

Twenty minutes later, when we were trying to remove the tyre, having phoned our roadside assistance people, a piece of luck turned up in the shape of a Renault rescue vehicle. (Ours is a Renault Megane.) The driver explained he had just been attending another incident a few kilometres back. "*No problema,*" he assured us as he changed the tyre expertly and cheerfully, refusing to take payment. This was just as well, as when I went to fetch my bag from the car so as to give him a few euros there was no bag and neither was my husband's equivalent- a German-style 'handtasche' – in its usual place. We wuz robbed!

What to do? Nothing we could do, but press on with our journey as best we could in a state of shock. Several hours later we were in the police station in Zarautz, telling our tale to the local *policia* with the help of a Basque couple who spoke good English and so could help our limited Spanish along. The young duty copper took everything down and made copies – this all took an hour and a half and we had not yet reported to our hotel, for which we had possessed a 50-euro voucher. 'Had' was the operative word as of course it was in the stolen handtasche. To add to our chagrin, said young copper gave us two copies of one sheet and nothing of the other he had produced. We really could not face going back to him – as long as HE had the necessary…

So, next stop the hotel. Another setback – the charming receptionist, though sympathetic, insisted she could not give us a room without the voucher or payment of the 50 euros over again. Nothing we could say would change the situation. Fortunately, although he had got away with most of our necessities, the highway robber had left me with my credit card – in my zipped jeans pocket.

Small mercies! And so, I was able to secure us a roof over our heads for the night, before the next day dawned with its myriad worries. First of these was the matter of our stolen passports, the means of getting back into our own country. We still had two overnight stops to make – luckily booked on 't'internet' but we had meals to pay for en route, for which expense my credit card could not be reliable. We had to use it to obtain ready cash – something we never do. "It's the commission, stupid!"

On went our journey until we reached Cherbourg, to face up the port officials regarding the passports. To our surprise and gratitude they were sympathetic – it seemed we were by no means the only people to be so inconvenienced and actually passport thefts had been very popular recently. "Do not worry, madame-m'sieur", the young woman reassured us: "we give you pieces of paper and all will be well!"

Six hours later and we were home, with all the other ramifications. First was to check on the report husband had made of his credit card loss – already missing two days- and second the passports. New applications must be made, with endorsements from character witnesses, meaning of course the need to explain what had occurred on the Spanish highway. We decided to tell as few of our relatives and friends as humanly possible, feeling we had gone and were going through enough hassle without too much more comment, however sympathetic! My choice of friend to help us our here was a good one, as she had recently been deprived of her handbag containing her own passport, plus credit card, driving licence and a wad of euros. We both agreed the charm of things Spanish had somewhat waned.

The effect of the credit card theft soon became apparent - the monthly statement arrived, looking very different from the usual record of four or five items of modest prices. Our little 'helper' had been busy – up and down the *autovias* spending our money, on petrol mainly and anywhere the card could be wiped and he could forge the signature. The total was over £100, spent on one day, which the bank agreed to write off. Six weeks later husband heard from the Visa Card people – a letter telling him that a 'fraud' status had been applied to his account and it had been closed, with immediate effect – the stolen card had been cancelled anyway, of course. Funny or what?

We returned to Spain in September, this time by air and hire car from the airport, where we looked all round us and drove with windows up and locked. There was a spate of bag thefts from people preoccupied with fetching cars and putting bags on the deck meanwhile. Had 'our' young criminal changed his modus operandi? We didn't wait to find out! One of our visits here was to the travel agent who had sold us the hotel voucher – remember that?

With this charming and efficient young woman we drew a blank. No amount of persuasion would alter her firm stance – she could not refund our 50 euros forked out for the stolen voucher, which presumably had languished unused, probably in a litter bin somewhere.

Notes On This N' That

East. West, home's best – even such confirmed Hispanophiles as Gerald Brenan concluded in the last chapter of his *Face of Spain* (written in 1950 after a ten year absence) that England "was a country worth belonging to". And a more recent traveller-cum-writer, the American Bill Bryson, maintains that England is the best place in which to live day-to-day. He cites our mail and newspaper deliveries – among other amenities.

The cranes are flying high – or rather swinging high and low as more and more building begins on many manifold sites. If we venture an enquiry like: *"Que es edificio aqui?"* the reply is invariably: *"No se!"* with a shrug of the shoulder or a beatific smile.

Ladies of short stature and uncertain age walk in the street, ignoring the paved sidewalks – and the growing number of vehicles (White van man abounds together with bulldozers, JCBs, cement mixers) at their peril.

Building on, building up – on it goes, the frantic altering and improving (sometimes this is a misnomer). The din is tremendous and unwelcome and it seems there is nothing we can do about it!

Not that we haven't tried. Visits to the *ayuntamiento* have become frequent and usually unproductive. I did have two successes. A streetlamp had been installed, thanks to the persistence of our Dutch neighbour, since returned to Holland. The electricians had left a gash across the road, waiting for more than a year to be filled in. My third plea to *el secretari* resulted in a bucketful of cement, spread across the road filling in the gash and another hole made by the marble men. And, we were suddenly, after two and a half years no longer in the Street with No Name. Carrer del Montgo it is now – defiantly Valenciano, not Calle Montgo in the Castilian Spanish of my classes.

Let Them Eat Bread!

We are exhorted frequently in the 'meeja' – especially near the season of goodwill – to take part in a 'shopping experience', in New York or some European city. Take your pick – Prague, Vienna, Berlin, anywhere but in your native land.

Let us tell you about the shopping experience in Benivergel – it really is something else! My husband takes up the story:

"Picture a man of mature years, more than six feet tall and broad shouldered with it, making his way down the main street – the grandly - named Calle Mayor, towards one of the two bakeries, El Forn. It is eight a.m. and it is worth mentioning that I am not a morning person until I have had my coffee and croissant. I am inside the shop and in front of me are four women, none over five feet in height – vertically challenged if you like – but what they lack in this respect they make up in the way they know best. They are short of stature but long of tongue.

"No one is actually in a queue. It's a gathering of the clans, with almost everyone related, typical still of many Spanish village communities.

"I wait upon the daily ritual of 'pan purchase', buying bread to you and me. They are going one-to-one with the baker's wife – it's verbal full flow." "Two more please", time for more chat- it's a free for all, with two or three more women on hand to join in. What we have here is the early morning verbal 'fix', with the menfolk at work or still in bed. A centuries-old ritual as fixed as the time of day.

"As I catch the eye of the baker's wife behind the narrow counter I may squeeze through the throng and offer: "*Pardon, buenos dias*", in my faltering Spanish. "*Dos croissants y un pan rustica, por favor*" I boom. Silence among the little ladies. Am I taking the bread from their mouths? Do they ponder how odd these foreigners are?

"I shall never know – such is my reprehensible lack of Spanish, partly excused by my wife's saying they have two languages – Castilian Spanish (similar to our BBC English) and Valenciano. And, the locals use a local dialect nobody understands anyway!"

Joys Of Banking

Banking in Spain is something else. One goes through a door marked 'paper trail'. Open an account in Banco Central Hispano and the avalanche of paper begins its silent roar. We were welcomed with a fulsome missive from the HQ in Madrid, informed that we were valuable and esteemed clients and advised that if we were to buy shares we would be eligible for such goodies as a ham – *jamon Serrano* – or a case of Rioja red, for example.

Together with current and deposit accounts we applied for a bank credit card so that we were not constantly raiding our UK account, using our NatWest Mastercard. This has resulted in the situation whereby for every purchase we make – a restaurant meal, a night in a hotel, fill-up at a petrol pump, a store purchase plus weekly supermarket forays – a piece of paper is issued.

These statements are on foolscap envelope-size pieces of paper and backed by a covering note of equal size. All those felled trees! Not only is this strange procedure carried out but also copious information is mailed to us each month on the state of our finances, again on separate pieces of paper. Electricity and water payments, rates and taxes (some imposed only on foreigners) – all are detailed.

So, added to the mountain of junk mail generated in this country – which I try valiantly to stop – is the pile from Espana. What have we done to deserve this treatment? We ask Ingrid, our pretty and patient adviser at BCH, if she could feed into their staff meetings our bewilderment and frustration. But, she shrugs her Swedish shoulders and just says: "I am sorry, but we are in Spain!"

We are tilting at windmills! The quixotic knight of La Mancha is in our thoughts as we open the latest missive from Madrid.

In the past Spaniards have been reluctant to hold bank accounts, preferring to hoard their (then) *pesetas* elsewhere – under their mattress? In recent years the savings banks like CAM (Caja *Ahorro Mediterraneo*) have sprung up, with branches in most small towns – smaller and more user-friendly than the larger more impersonal Banco de Valencia and or BCH. Can we dare to hope that with this sea-change in Spanish habits we may see as well as famous national dislike of officialdom and regulations – a change in banking procedures? I fervently hope so!

Avian Games

One evening, back in the day, before the ruination of 'our' village, we looked up and saw a strange, nay even bizarre, sight.

A flock of birds were overhead – in itself not an unusual occurrence – but these had plumage of variegated hues, ranging through the spectrum, like a rainbow in flight. What was going on? *Que?*

The birds darted and swooped hither and thither, but then we began to discern a sort of pattern. One of the number was plainly 'dressed', its feathers ordinary brown. In the usual way of the species, was this one female? Assuming this to be so, she was being chased by the others, about twenty of them, at a fast and furious rate.

Next day we asked our neighbour Terry, a full-time resident of 18 years, what was the ritual enacted with such enthusiasm? "Oh," he replied," that's the battle of the sexes or, you might say, a sex game! The males do indeed chase the hen and the first to catch her is the winner."

He told us that the Bar Julio round the corner was the headquarters of the society, which met there weekly. We popped in for a glass of wine and sure enough on their wall were numerous pictures, in full colour, of the mobile aviary, seen in the sky a couple of days before. The winged contestants were kept in cages on top of an apartment block in the next street. This was an early model and therefore part of the landscape, before the new ones had been even dreamed up.

The following week, on the same day, we kept watch and were rewarded with another display in glorious Technicolour. A different, rather charming custom – not as bloodthirsty as bullfighting, incidentally on its way out in many Spanish cities.

Building Blocks

We had made good time from the airport since a traumatic entry via seriously undermanned passport control point – one man to receive two planeloads, one of them containing numerous children who complained vociferously on our behalf to no avail. The upside was that our plane's baggage recovery carousel was just around the corner and our one suitcase came off at speed.

With thoughts of groceries in our minds (no meals on board the 'cheapos'), we fondly imagined we would stock up in the nearest *supermercado*, the French Intermarche – open until 9pm. This was not to be. Poised to turn in to the car park, we noticed the usual flags flying but there was nothing else – no large store. It was as if there had been a Wizard of Oz-type tornado – no Dorothy around though.

The next day, after finding a store open in the next village, we were told an arsonist had set a match to a pile of cardboard boxes and the whole edifice had gone up in flames. Rumours abounded of an insurance scam with no indication of rebuilding. '*Mañana*' had taken over!

Our next shock was nearer home. We knew from our neighbour that terrace conversions were afoot and also that a father and son were building a house opposite ours – a weekend and evening project. What we were not expecting was the construction of a four-storey apartment block on the next corner, just 200 metres away. All this activity meant noise from around 7.30am for at least 12 hours, except for their coffee breaks and lunch times. If lucky, we could expect a period of one and a half to two hours' peace for *siesta*. If not so lucky, someone could have an afternoon cement or marble delivery – then it was 'goodbye *siesta*'!

We were where we said we would never be – in the middle of a building site in an abnormally hot June due to air from the Sahara Desert.

Pros And Cons

One of the half-dozen villages nestling in the Val de Rectoria 'our' village, Benivergel has an electronic newscast display in the town hall square. Flashing across in bright red are details of opening times – post office, library, police station and information desk – with the date and exact time plus temperature in Centigrade.

This modernity sits oddly with the backwardness and neglect in other respects – dilapidated dwellings, damaged roads with huge jagged potholes a danger to suspension, rotting tyres, dust and litter all over the place.

We had begun to realise that, of course, the village had to change and there would be no halting the march of progress towards modernity.

The mayor and his council had built the *ayuntamiento* (town hall) as a millennium project, with the library following two years later. The new Policia Local station (staffed with four personnel, three men and one woman) appeared between the two buildings.

Ergo, a larger settlement was on the cards. A population of 1,600 (the 2001 figure) did not merit such magnificent edifices. And so the die was cast, the writing was on the wall, and any other clichés that come to mind.

To us retired Brits the massive change is unwelcome. We liked the old, traditional village with its seven bars, two bakeries, two butchers, one bank and the post office – open from 11 am until 1.30 pm, after the postmistress had done her rounds. Two hairdressers made livings also. We were fond of the little old village houses with their tiny wrought iron balconies, supporting pot upon pot of geraniums and petunias. Yes, some admittedly a bit ramshackle, their owners/tenants not the most sophisticated of beings, but friendly and inoffensive.

Crime has been almost unknown, just one bag snatch, not by a local, in five years. Just as unknown are lager louts. The Spanish like their wine and some of the men, old and young, drink beer but not to excess even in soaring summer temperatures. The term 'binge-drinking' is incomprehensible to them.

And so, there were things we should miss, but overall we felt a sense of disappointment. All matters considered, we did not want to stay. We put the house on the market and returned to England. Three months passed with no sniff of a buyer and we began to have second thoughts. Owning a second home abroad had become part of our lifestyle – we would miss the journeys to and from the village, visiting places en route in Spain and France we would otherwise never have encountered.

By this time it was New Year 2006. Maybe a new beginning? Off the market came the house and we reverted to the usual pattern. But, a year later the situation had worsened, with building everywhere. Every corner where there had been a workshop or large old house was now a construction site.

"Site Rep" 2006

And so, *adios los marmoles*! After four years, the marble workshop opposite our little house is closing down and moving lock, stock and barrel to the industrial estate, two kilometres away on the outskirts of the village.

After the usual Spanish fashion, they are late – it is now March. The Hockney-loving secretary man had told us firmly, back in the autumn that "they must move in December". We arrived on 28 February to see no change. But what's this? Four days on and a lorry with crane arrived. Massive slabs of granite were heaved on to said lorry until we feared for the axles – slabs black, green, mottled and even orange, matching the fruit on the nearby trees!

Lorry and crane kept going back and forth all day and the next morning (Sunday). No rest on the seventh day for these boys. We held out hopes for an imminent evacuation to be ready for the inevitable construction site, to comply with the current policy of the *ayuntamiento* – to fill every square metre in this small town.

Return trips for more marble continued spasmodically over the next two weeks, with a combination crane-cum-lorry brought into operation. With extraordinary precision a gaping hole was created by the huge and heavy stabiliser lowered from the back of the vehicle. This new hole was a companion to the even larger one already in situ, made shortly after the tarmac surface had been laid four years previously. Not good news for motorists at all.

Move on six months and *plus ça change, plus ça la meme chose* (excuse the lapse into French). Holes not filled in, also unsightly gash still across the road – legacy from electricians when they installed street lights.

OK, another visit to the *ajuntament*.

And...Later That Year

And so, we are back to the heat and dust of the 'war zone' that is the village in summer. On every corner is a building site or one in waiting- 'ripe for development' is the time honoured phrase.

We wonder why such a rush? Why is each spare square metre being filled with cement ready for yet more apartment blocks, all at the same time? The answer was given inadvertently by Javier, the charming secretary to the council. Yes, the Hockney Fan.

When telling us that the site of the defunct marble factory – now removed to the *poligono industriel* – had been sold to a developer, he let drop that new regulations were to be brought in, ruling that heed must be paid to the aesthetics of a building project.

Architecture and general appearance were to become important. But, not yet! So, the plans for 26 two-bedroomed apartments to be put up there had only to be approved by the architect, who probably designed them anyway.

This admission could explain the sense of urgency around the place – and undoubtedly does!

Progress?

Our arrival in mid-June 2006 after an absence of nearly four months was dramatic to say the least. We had been warned by our good neighbour Annie that we would see some changes in the village. She wasn't kidding!

As we approached our street in darkness we saw it, illuminated in our headlights – a three-metre high heap of earth and rubble, dwarfing the nearest house, a small stone property of many summers. Next morning we saw that the heap was not only high but broad and long, stretching for 15 metres along the *barranca* (a ravine-like area at one time cultivated by owners of the ancient dwellings on the opposite side).

It was market day, so on our way to buy fruit and veg we dropped into the Town Hall for a word or several with *el secretari*, (he who loves Hockney prints). "*Que es?*" we asked him, briefly and to the point.

The heap had been imported from elsewhere, i.e. a building site where dredging out had been done before the dreaded pile-driving and then cement-filling stages. The purpose of the heap was to fill in the *barranca* preparatory to building yet more houses, a terrace of 14 plus parking spaces. *Quel horreur*!

Worse was yet to come. By the start of July the filling-in process had begun, involving lorries and, most noisy of all contraptions, a steam roller complete with beeper. Beepers are compulsory attachments on all vehicles when reversing, as a safety precaution. And so, every time the roller moved backwards – every few minutes – off went the beeper.

As is usual for Spanish workmen, the assault on our senses began at 7.30 after which time sleep was impossible. One of the pleasures of our second home is to emerge on to the spacious first floor terrace, for our morning tea and later for coffee or drinks. Needless to say, this was no longer a sensible option. Perversely, when we had reached 9.30 am without insanity setting in, they all decamped for their breakfast – filling up the village bars for the next hour or so. Then, 'the noise, my dear, and the people' would recommence.

No Regrets – At October 2005

Since our return from Spain 10 days ago we have taken out four books from the local library, bought and planted two dozen bedding plants from a nearby garden centre, watched several interesting programmes on digital TV, been to the cinema and booked seats for a second visit.

Tomorrow we are off to London, saying to hell with the evil malcontents who blew up fifty people on 7/7. I want to see the George Stubbs exhibition at the Tate and my other half the Iraq war exhibit at the Army Museum. We shall board a red bus to travel between the two buildings.

After our cultural morning we shall lunch at the 'Angel and Crown', a traditional pub on the Charing Cross Road near the Actors' Church (another favourite place), on their superb fish and chips. Then we'll have a look around the National and National Portrait Galleries before sinking into a teashop in one of these great establishments.

This account of very typical 'touristy' activities sums up the reasons why we could never live in Spain full-time. At one time a few years back we had thought we would do just that, but now – as Maggie Thatcher asserted: "No, no, no!"

Great to visit their wonderful cities and some of their very scenic areas and there are some terrific restaurants and excellent wines, but they can keep the rest! I am convinced that vast numbers of migrants from our rainy island – or green and pleasant land – do regret burning their boats and do miss their homeland. They don't want to lose face and so remain in a half-life with its cheap wine, many bars and coffee shops and the various clubs run by Brits for ex-pat Brits. Some folk throw themselves into charity work and this is commendable, but isn't there plenty of that here at home, where it is said "charity begins"?

The *Saga* magazine runs regular features about ex-pats in different foreign parts. These brave souls are always asked "What do you miss?" The lists – sometimes lengthy – convince me that they are not in such an idyllic spot and might just as well return to their native land. Sunshine – and you can have too much – is not worth the hassle.

Remembering 'Barca'

Now that we are well away from the village that became a large building site with its heat and dust – in wet weather mud – we can allow time for memories. Now that we have turned our back on the place that used to hold such allure, we can remember some of the attractions that held us for those years.

Our visits to Madrid, Barcelona and Valencia – Spain's Big Three, each with their individual seductiveness: 'Barca' came top with us – the city had so much to offer and much of it free too. The Rambla must be one of the most enchanting streets in the world – the living statues, the teeming flower stalls, the pavement cafes and bars and the Gaudi-dominated newsstands. Halfway down is the Mercat Bocqueria, the largest covered market in Spain, its stalls unbelievable in their plentiful produce, staffed by cheerful and colourfully dressed sellers, many in regional costume and all in good voice! Always worth a visit even if not buying much.

At the sea end of the Rambla is the Cristobal Colon (Columbus to you and me) statue, appropriately looking out to sea and marking the beginning of the attractive Mare Magnum development, dating from the Olympic Games of 1992. Just a good place for sauntering around gulping the ozone, or taking to the water in one of the passenger craft.

Easily reached by train from Valencia, in its turn reached from the village by a half-hour drive to a train station with a secure car park and thence by a 45-minute journey, the city abounds in attractions. Several museums include the tiny Shoe Museum near the Cathedral, where I was intrigued to find the original 'Hotter' design – as worn by no less a personage then Christopher Columbus (or Cristobal Colon) himself. Made from one piece of leather, the flat, round-toed shoe with one wide strap and square buckle was exactly like the pair I was wearing that day!

The Museo Picasso is in the old quarter, the Barri Gotti. Pablo was, of course, a Spaniard by birth though French by adoption – from Malaga to Paris at the age of 19. His most famous works are in Madrid, in the Reina Sofia gallery, but in Barcelona are some of his most charming sketches.

The old city had enjoyed a renaissance since its staging of the Olympic Games in 1992. The docks area underwent a dramatic transformation, becoming a gastronomic honey pot, with upmarket seafood restaurants replacing the old beach bars. Their regular clients are the owners of the luxury apartments in the soaring blocks supplanting the fishermen's abodes of yesteryear.

The long road bisecting the city, the Avenida Diagonal, has been lengthened further to reach the sea and a new district has sprung up encompassing a conference centre, shopping mall and yet more 1uxury flats. The excellent Metro system has been extended – for speeding the occupants to their occupations.

But the name that dominates 'Barca' is Antoni Gaudi, the gifted, modest man whose amazing structures have enchanted visitors to the city for decades. His unfinished Sagrada Familia, begun a century ago, became his home for many months before his sudden death in 1926, under the wheels of a tram. His star had waned so much that he was not recognised and was buried without ceremony. For a long while his little packet of sandwiches hung from a rafter in the yet-to-be completed structure. Not to be missed: Casa Batllo, La Pedrera, Palau – but how to choose? All are fascinating.

We became very fond of Barcelona, making several visits during our sojourn in the province of Valencia – by rail from Xeraco, a station with a large (free) car park. We had been assured of the safety aspect there, and so it proved to be on the four occasions we left our vehicle for as long as four nights.

And so, we were soon familiar with all that the city had to offer – cultural attractions plus sybaritic charms like the delicious repasts in the superb fish restaurants along the quayside. We loved the eatery in the Maritime Museum, the only drawback its erratic opening hours!

To add to the reasons for our pilgrimages to 'Barca' besides the art galleries, museums and atmospheric bars like Picasso's haunt 'Las Quatre Gats' we discovered a marvellous addition to our entertainment there – a Yelmo multi complex. Ten cinemas, some large, some small, showing- joy of joys, British and American movies in 'V.O.'- original version.

These films thus served a dual purpose- the dialogue in our native tongue was (mostly) comprehensible and the Spanish sub-titles assisted our 'skill' with their *lingua franca*. Among these cinematic delights were Cate Blanchett as Elizabeth 1, 'The Village', 'Mr and Mrs Smith', 'Monster-in-Law' and many others.

The journey there from Placa Catalunya on the 41 bus became as familiar as the Red Arrow from Waterloo Station to my office in Horseferry Road. We would wait at the stop opposite El Corte Ingles along with housewives laden with goods, students laden with books and commuters laden with laptops and mobile phones – all bound for the new developments on the edge of the city. The cinema complex stood as part of a shopping mall in a street lined with apartment blocks, sprinkled with trendy restaurants and boutiques. If we were feeling especially flush, we would have a pre- or post-film supper in the local Mexican.

B&B Spanish Style

A necessary part of our journeying in Spain was, of course, somewhere to lay our heads as we ate up the kilometres. Someone told us about *los paradores de turismo*. Founded in 1928 and opened by King Alfonso XIII, these mostly ancient buildings are well established as hotels throughout the country.

We stayed in 11 paradors altogether, during those seven years of driving back and forth from ports in Spain to our house in the Marina Alta region. From the 'blurb' at the beginning of their directory, *los paradores* guard Spain's national and artistic heritage while promoting quality tourism and dynamising those regions with few economic advantages.

They varied from those steeped in antiquity to upstart modernity but common to all was the high standard of comfort and excellent cuisine. If fault were to be found it was with the lateness of the dining hour, 8.30 pm was common. Spaniards have no problem with this, but we Anglo-Saxons, including Germans and Dutch besides we Brits, found our digestions suffering.

On one memorable evening the kitchen staff in the Calahorra *parador* had been rushed off their feet coping with a wedding feast. At 8.30 pm, the appointed dinner time, there was no sign of anything approaching service. Ten minutes later a weary waiter emerged to take orders for the first course. At 9.15 we were served with soup and other 'starters'. The 'mains' arrived half an hour later, by which time many of the clientele had fallen asleep! Several glasses of wine had been imbibed during the long wait.

What had also happened during that time was the loss of patience suffered by a group of Germans, six-strong, who at 9 pm stormed the door to the kitchen. Otherwise, the 9.15 soup might have been even later...

The episode was a pity, as it marred our enjoyment of the 60-bedroom parador, a lovely red-brick mansion, situated at the end of a long garden running the length of the town's main street. The town lies on the plains of the river Ebro and is within the old kingdom of Navarra, linked to Aragon to its east. The region is very fertile, especially for grapevines producing the Rioja red wine.

Calahorra is rich in churches and has a fine Cathedral as well as convent and a Bishop's Palace. The restaurant's menu features regional dishes using Rioja wines. In the centre of the area, in the Alava region, is the 55-bedroom Parador Hotel Argomaniz. This is a Renaissance palace, where Napoleon Bonaparte rested before attacking Vitoria-Gasteiz during the Peninsular Wars.

At that time the palace was owned by the Larrea family, whose cost of arms adorns the building's façade. Vitoria is an easy eight-kilometer journey by local bus and is well worth visiting, with an old quarter several museums and two other palaces besides a cathedral and some interesting old houses. Outdoor interests can be satisfied by a nature reserve, a natural park and the reservoirs of the Gorbea mountains.

The oldest Parador out of the 11 we experienced must be the Castillo de Siguenza, a twelfth-century medieval castle. This edifice, begun in 1123, is installed in a Moorish Citadel built on a Roman settlement. Bishops and cardinals dwelt here until the beginning of the twentieth century. On high ground and a very imposing structure, it is equally splendid inside, especially the dining room with its huge proportions and high beamed ceiling. The menu on offer is appropriate, including game and roast kid dishes.

At the Parador de Almagro, a sixteenth-century Franciscan convent in La Mancha, typical cooking of that region is offered in the Louis XV dining room. In Avila a vegetable and pork stew or roast suckling pig can be sampled, as well as 'yemas de Saint Teresa', a desert.

Travel to the Route of the Three Kings and Tortosa's Parador and you will find 'anguila en suc' (eels in juice) or 'suquet de peix' (fish in sauce); move on to the Maestrazgo Route and the Parador de Teruel and you will be able to eat lamb stew and a special cheese and egg dessert.

I almost forgot one of the real gems – Cuenca, in the autonomous community of Castile-La Mancha. The town is built across a steep spur, from which slopes descend into deep gorges of the Jucar and Huecar rivers.

In 714 Muslim Arabs captured the area, realized how strategically based was the location and built a fortress called Kunka. This new city became prosperous from agriculture and textile manufacturing.

Fast forward through centuries to 1093 when, after years of battles, Christian troops entered the city only to lose it 15 years later. Eventually in 1177 Arab domination was ended by the young King Alfonso VIII of Castile (son-in-law of Henry II and Eleanor of Aquitaine).

For about 500 years Cuenca flourished, until Napoleon's Peninsular Wars reduced the population to 6,000. The arrival of the railway in the 19th century meant a boost to 10,000 people. Came the civil war and Franco took the city in 1938, bringing in another period of decline. In recent years tourism has helped the city, so much so that it was declared a World Heritage site in 1996 and is to apply to be the European City of Culture in 2016.

The Parador, where we spent two nights, is situated on lower ground than much of the city, opposite the *Casas Colgadas* (Hanging Houses). These dwellings cling to the side of the Huecar gorge and have been there since the 15th century. Refurbished in the 1920s, one is now a restaurant and another the *Museo de Arte Abstracto Espanol*.

Some of these unusual hotels are a little tricky to find and they have their quirks, but how much more rewarding we found them than the safe, predictable modern 'chain' places. Go find!

Serendipity in Sagunto

A Proustian moment occurred a few days ago, as I was listening to a radio programme featuring Hannibal and his epic crossing of the Alps, complete with elephants. It seems he had made a stopover in Saguntum, a Roman settlement on the Levant coast or better known as the Bay of Valencia.

Back in the day, 'BB' before Benivergel, we made a property search along the Costa del Azahar (the Orange Blossom Coast). We did not buy, mainly because of a flash of insight we foresaw a building boom in that area. How right we were – some of the formerly small resorts now resemble mini-Manhattans.

However, we did visit some of the attractions and one of these was the now-named Sagunto. We drove there from our hotel in Valencia in a hired car and duly found a car park, then set off to see the sights.

According to information displayed in the church of Santa Maria, Sagunto began life in the fifth century BC, as a walled settlement overlooking the plain below. It had its own Mint and traded with Greek and Phoenician colonies and by 219 was large and prosperous, in which year it was captured by Hannibal. It was not pacified by Rome but rather given favoured status together with several Roman buildings, including the theatre. Build in the first century using the concave shape of the mountain; it has wonderful acoustics and seating areas for 6,000 spectators, the façade being about 90 metres in length. It has undergone an extensive restoration and is used for a three-week, open-air August arts festival.

The castle, almost a kilometre long, rebuilt from the original Roman by the Moors, preserves part of the forum, cisterns, walls, basilica, curia and the 'tabernae'. Down the hill we found the arcaded square which leads to the Jewish Quarter, with its narrow streets of whitewashed houses and pointed arches. On the Calle Mayor (main street) are some splendid mansions. Near the church are the remains of the Temple of Diana – the only edifice left untouched by Hannibal. Remains of the circus (2nd – 3rd century AD) are preserved, also the bridge over the Palencia river.

Out explorations had given us an appetite and we looked for somewhere to eat lunch. Oddly, there were only a couple of restaurants open – it was a Monday, not a good day. But, we did choose well as rabbit stew was on the menu and very good it was too, accompanied by crusty rolls and the house red. So fortified, we went on our way.

Away from the history and cultural attractions, we found the port and sandy beaches, proudly flying the Blue Flag. Then, a serendipitous discovery! We noticed a poster advertising the Caves of San Jose and followed the directions, to find a hidden gem. It was an underground river, actually the longest navigable one in Europe. We were seated in a wooden boat with four other people and taken through the caves back and forth, observing odd rock formations and stalactites and stalagmites until we came upon a lake. It was an amazing experience and one only found by accident, serendipity indeed!

Back to the car park, but where was the car? We could not (a) remember where we put it and (b) remember what it looked like! Consternation set in, until husband realised he had a piece of paper in his pocket, which might 'give us a clue'... The said piece of paper told us it was a Toyota Yaris, but no other info. That was something, so our search began. It turned out, after 20 minutes' trudging about in the hot sun among heaps of metal, that we had left the car at the very edge of the car park, in the farthest corner. There must have been some reason, but it had escaped us. And so the day ended with our drive back to Valencia and our modern hotel, but we did not forget easily our sojourn in Sagunto and out boat ride underground.

Gallery

Holy Family façade, Gaudi's new cathedral Sagrada Familia (unfinished)

More Gaudi – chimneys on Casa Mila

And again – ceramic lizard, Parc Guell

Carnival in Barcelona with animals

Traditional giant figures – 'gegants' (farmer's wife in centre)

Goodness and naughtiness!

'Cutting edge' shop – scissors, knives etc

The largest sweetshop in Spain

Valencia's town hall, a former palace

Ronda's El Tajo gorge

Bell tower on Santa Maria, Ronda – former mosque

Frigiliana – mountain village near Nerja

Lemon tree, Benivergel near our house

www.ingramcontent.com/pod-product-compliance
Lightning Source LLC
Chambersburg PA
CBHW061952070426
42450CB00007BA/1355